Funnel Building

B. Vincent

Published by RWG Publishing, 2021.

FUNNEL BUILDING

First edition. July 14, 2021.

Written by B. Vincent.

Also by B. Vincent

Bridge Pages
Business Acquisition
Business Bogging
Marketing Automation
Better Meetings
Conversion Optimization
Creative Solutions
Employee Recruitment
Startup Capital
Employee Mentoring
Servant Leadership
Human Resources
Team Building
Funnel Building

Table of Contents

Funnel Building

Welcome to this seminar on pipe building. In this course, we will cover how to assemble viable deals pipes for your business. This course is isolated into three modules. Module one covers arranging and picking your pipe type, module two covers making and fragmenting your offers, and module three covers making the pipe pages themselves. When this course is finished, you'll realize how to viably assemble channels that create leads and deals for your business. So right away, we should plunge into the main module.

Module One

Welcome to module one. In this module, our master will show you arranging and picking your channel type. Thus, prepare to take a few notes, and how about we bounce directly in.

So we'll utilize Click Funnels for this preparation since it's ostensibly the most notable and broadly utilized stage out there. The primary thing we will do is examine every one of the various types of pipes there are to look over, and afterward we'll design our own. As you can see there's no deficiency of kinds of pipes you can construct. We have imperceptible channels which comprise of content being conveyed first, and afterward requesting installment on the following page, on the off chance that they preferred it, very few have known about that one. We have Video Sales Letter Funnel that are intensely dependent on deals recordings. We have Lead Magnet Funnels where you're offering something for nothing, as a trade-off for an email select in. We have Reverse Squeeze Page pipes which convey content first and afterward request an email pick in one more exceptional sort. We have the two-venture tripwire that permits you to pitch a low ticket offer, trailed by upsells. We have the Bridge Funnel where you gather a lead, and afterward move them on to another pipe like an offshoot offer. We have a Sales Letter Funnel, a more customary channel comprising of long-structure deals pages. We have Auto Webinar, and a live online course enrollment and participation pipes, incredible in case you're selling high ticket things. We have Hero Funnels that genuinely stress your own image. Overview Funnels where you can study your guests and afterward divert them to an offer dependent on their answers. Ask Campaign Funnels, a moving sort that assists you with sorting out what your crowd needs. Landing page Funnels which are intended to kind of copy the part of conventional sites, yet channel individuals into your offers. Application Funnels are incredible for qualifying likely instructing or high ticket administration customers. Every day Deal Funnels are tied in with getting new clients with overpowering offers. Participation Funnels are intended to sell items and get individuals into your individuals' regions. The Product Launch Funnel, a progression of video pages intended to prepare individuals for a major dispatch by the end, spearheaded by Jeff Walker, obviously. Live Demo Funnels are incredible for exhibiting and demoing your items or administrations. Customer facing facade Funnels are intended to copy the look and feel of a web based business store prior to piping individuals through to your center offers. Culmination Funnels, ideal for getting large names together in one online occasion. Dropping Funnels, an incredible method to attempt to hold individuals back from escaping, just as realizing why they needed to. Also, the Squeeze Page Funnel, a select in pipe that use the force of ultra moderation and interest to get pick ins.

Presently, in case you're overpowered, relax, you don't have to stress over by far most of these yet. In case you're simply beginning with channels or simply beginning with business online as a rule, there's just a modest bunch you truly need to stress over. By the day's end, it relies upon what you have and how you need to offer it to the world. All in all, do you have a book, a digital book? Do you have a video course? Do you have information that could without much of a stretch be transformed into a book or video course? Do you have a high ticket offer that you need to sell through a long online class show? Of the things you have, would you like to part with one of them free of charge for lead age, which one? For our motivations, I think we'll say we're pursuing the most available and normal situation. We have an unconditional present, and we have an item we need to charge cash for. Presently for that kind of channel, I'm really going to click up here on exemplary pipe manufacturer.

I'll click sell my item, and I'll pick ordinary deals channel.

I'll give it a name.

Also, I'll hit assemble channel. However, before we really get into that before we begin planning the channel. We need to begin sorting out, of the things we have, what would we like to part with for nothing? What's more, what would we like to sell? That is all essential for creating in fragmenting, which is the thing that we will cover in the following module.

Module 2

Hello people, welcome to module two. In this module, our master will tell you the best way to art and splinter your offers. So prepare to take a few notes, and we should hop directly in.

Alright folks, so this will be a smidgen on the fly. There's a great deal of conceptualizing going on here. We're checking out what we have. Also, we need to sort out how we can make an offer or a pipe of different offers, in light of what we have available to us. You need to get somewhat imaginative here now and then. For our situation, we need one thing to part with, and one thing to sell. We have a lot of digital books to cover a few subjects: item dispatches, group the board, minimal expense startup. We got video courses here, which have high seen esteem and would almost certainly be something to be thankful for to sell at a low to mid ticket cost, as our upsell after someone picks in. We've likewise got a couple of random things here that we've sorted as others. Presentation page formats, those could be helpful individuals may pay for those that additionally perhaps something great to part with for nothing as a lead magnet. Deals page investigates, that is a decent one, an important one kind of a one on a certain something, so that is most likely something we would charge a superior cost for. Same thing with training.

Presently, this is the thing that we have available to us.

What's more, one thing that I end up having here on my hard drive is this one here, a video course called High-Level Mastermind. Presently I'll really maneuver that onto this slide down here to make sure we can see it and envision it, and it is actually what it says. OK, it's a long video course that discussions about more significant level techniques that can kind of take your business to a higher level, it's an extremely helpful video course. Presently, here's the inquiry. Do we need to go into our sack of things and discover a lower ticket thing to part with free of charge, that is applicable?

We most likely could. I mean a portion of these may be applicable or we could go out and purchase or permit something different. In any case, I recall that this one incorporates a little PDF guide, that kind of frameworks the course and kind of hits the central matters. Presently it's anything but promoted here as a component of its kind of an idea in retrospect, I surmise, anyway it's anything but a helpful PDF guide. So the inquiry is, do we need to essentially to make a proposal for this pipe, alright a two-section offer something free of charge and something to sell, do we need to fundamentally proceed to snatch another thing to add to this, or would we be able to accomplish something many refer to as fragmenting. On the off chance that we as of now have a segment of this offer that is applicable to this offer. Would it be smarter to take that part out and stick it here as the section point as the free giveaway?

By and large, yes and that is known as an item fragmenting or offer fragmenting now we don't have an approach to publicize that PDF. So the thing we will do is get somewhat inventive here, and we will make an ecover. Alright, so we really have something to put on our business page in our channel that makes it look sort of pleasant.

In this way, how about we please here to my ecover maker.com extraordinary instrument for making designs, to give your information item kind of a substantial vibe. Also, we will get this iPad here, so it's useful for addressing digital books and PDFs, and we should feel free to look, pictures, and how about we search for business people.

A few decent ones here. I like this one with a person composing something on a whiteboard that sounds similar to driving forces. Isn't that right?

Land, so we'll get that arranged there.

I'm really going to make that somewhat more modest.

And afterward we should put a title up top, and how about we simply kind of call it something almost identical. OK, it doesn't need to be precisely the same title. We'll call it significant level techniques.

Feel free to resize that a tad. What's more, that looks fine alright, that resembles a decent digital book or a decent free report to part with. We'll click Finalize, we'll give two or three minutes to deliver that. Furthermore, there you go, that is not an awful looking digital book or an awful looking PDF. OK, we presumably might have made it's anything but somewhat prettier. Alright, this could be somewhat more flush, I surmise, however you get the thought OK we took something that as of now exists, inside the resources that we have inside the offer, the primary center thing that we will sell. We took a part, and we fragmented it away from it and made it kind of its own independent thing. Alright, and we will use this present, how about we feel free to download this dab png record, we will use this, in our channel. So return here, drag this right in here to have the option to envision what we're discussing. What we will wind up doing is sending traffic to a section point, where we offer this free of charge, OK.

After we offer that free of charge. We will send them to this, where we charge a specific value we haven't chose at this point, for this video course, OK. What we gathered here, when we parted with this free of charge, be that as it may, was messages. OK, so we will send individuals into an arrangement of computerized messages, probably.

It's quite possibly the most essential channels, so regardless of whether no one purchases the item that you wound up selling here, basically you wound up getting a lead added to your email list. OK, so this is practically it folks, this is the thing that it comes down to when you're contemplating either making offers, or fragmenting offers that you have into numerous parts that can make up different strides within a business channel. So since we have the thought, this is the thing that we're going for, our free segment, and our paid segments, we should feel free to take this present, how about we return into Clickfunnels, and how about we really go through the channel, planning measure where we really make the pages and get this going and sprung up.

Module 3

Okay, welcome to module three. In this module, our master will show you making the channel pages themselves. So prepare to take a few notes, and how about we hop directly in.

Alright, so in the event that you several exercises back, we have recently picked the pipe type and hit the catch, assemble my channel.

All things considered, this is the latest relevant point of interest. We picked this fundamental deals pipe with a free proposal at the section point, trailed by a business page with a paid item. Since we got done with creating and fragmenting our offer. We can begin really planning the pages. So first we'll have to pick a format for our lead page, there's a huge load of great ones here, yet I'm somewhat of a moderate person.

So I will pick this basic one, here.

Okay, since that is added to the pipe, we'll hit Edit page.

What's more, here, we should simply connect our picture and our duplicate. So we should tap on this book here.

I'll feel free to erase that.

I love this little bolt thing here, however don't think it'll jive well with our ecover. So I will erase this also.

I'll click this in addition to fasten to add a component.

Also, I'll pick picture.

Then, at that point I'll tap the picture placeholder.

Also, I'll come here and click on this picture button over on the right.

Also, I'll get our little digital book realistic that we made in the past exercise.

Alright, no issues up until now.

Presently we should simply add our duplicate a smidgen.

I'll double tap the feature and how about we supplant that with this feature for our lead magnet.

Also, we could utilize this subheadline here yet I don't think we'll require it so I'll erase that too.

Furthermore, I'd say we're good to go. How about we hit save, and afterward exit and continue ahead to the subsequent stage.

So our following stage is our business page.

Presently, I have very little duplicate for a long-structure direct mail advertisement, nor do I have a video. So I will bounce down to the base and select this decent short-structure moderate one.

Well that is stacked in our channel, I'll hit Edit page.

What's more, the primary thing we'll do is we'll begin supplanting this duplicate.

So I have a couple of lines ready here.

I'll embed this one here.

Also, this one here.

Also, this one here.

Also, this one down here.

Then, I'll feel free to begin erasing a portion of the components we don't require with the end goal of this model.

This segment.

This section can go.

This section.

This top menu bar.

Furthermore, we'll feel free to leave our companion Bill Newsum there and simply imagine it's a genuine statement from a genuine individual.

We'll tap on our picture placeholder here.

We'll tap the picture button on the right.

Also, we'll supplant it with our fundamental tabletop picture.

We'll do likewise down here with this one, tick the picture catch, and double tap this one.

Also, we'll do likewise down here with this one, tick on a picture button on the right, and double tap this one.

Also, the absolute last thing to do here is prepare our catch.

I'll change the catch text to purchase now.

Also, for set activity, we need to really mention to Clickfunnels what the catches will do since the request structure is the following hard-coded step in our channel. We can in a real sense simply pick, go to following stage in channel, directly down here.

Furthermore, we're good to go.

I'll hit Save.

Furthermore, in some cases it'll ask you for SEO metadata or I'll simply glue whatever was rearward in the clipboard here for the time being.

Furthermore, we'll hit Exit.

What's more, how about we return to our channel outline.

The subsequent stage is the request structure.

We'll click here and select a format.

There are huge loads of great ones to browse here. I for one like the antiquated thin request structure.

So we'll pick that one.

When that is prepared we'll click Edit page.

Also, there's not actually a lot to change on this one. I think I'll dispose of the logo.

What's more, we'll embed some new duplicate in this feature here.

Since thing name says progressively refreshed on the grounds that it is. At the point when we determine the item name somewhere else within Clickfunnels, it will be refreshed and pondered this structure, consequently, so there's nothing else to do here.

We should hit Save and Exit.

Then, we'll click on request affirmation.

Indeed, a lot of cool formats to look over. I will pick this blue mother channel one here.

What's more, whenever that is added, we'll click Edit Page.

Truly, the solitary thing to do here on this one is erase this logo. This is the place where individuals can see an affirmation of what they just purchased. Also, there's an entrance buy connect, which will take them to the thank you page which is the last advance in the channel.

So how about we click Save and Exit.

Lastly, how about we click on thank you page.

Presently, this is the last advance and it'll generally incorporate a download interface or an enrollment page or something to that effect.

We utilize this blue, much obliged, browse your email one down here on the left.

We'll click Edit page.

Furthermore, this is essentially all set with no guarantees. I'll simply erase this one additional line here in light of the fact that I don't have any duplicate for that and I don't think we need any. And afterward we'll have to mention to Clickfunnels what we need this catch to do.

So we'll click Set Action.

Also, we will just put the entrance URL here, regardless of whether it's anything but a direct download connect or an enrollment structure, for individuals to make a login to get to a part's region or anything like that.

I'm simply going to put, click funnels.com here for smiles.

We should hit Save and Exit one last time.

Also, the writing is on the wall, we've recently made our whole deals channel. From the passage point, which was a free offer, through a business page for a paid offer.

And afterward the request structure request affirmation, and thank you page where we can at long last convey that item to our new clients, and we're prepared to send traffic into this, we'll simply tap on deals page, which is the primary page in our pipe, and we can send them into this URL here.

Don't miss out!

Visit the website below and you can sign up to receive emails whenever B. Vincent publishes a new book. There's no charge and no obligation.

https://books2read.com/r/B-A-QWUO-JJLQB

BOOKS 2 READ

Connecting independent readers to independent writers.

Also by B. Vincent

Affiliate Marketing
Affiliate Marketing
Affiliate Marketing

Standalone
Affiliate Recruiting
Business Layoffs & Firings
Business and Entrepreneur Guide
Business Remote Workforce
Career Transition
Project Management
Precision Targeting
Professional Development
Strategic Planning
Content Marketing
Imminent List Building
Getting Past GateKeepers
Banner Ads
Bookkeeping

Bridge Pages
Business Acquisition
Business Bogging
Marketing Automation
Better Meetings
Conversion Optimization
Creative Solutions
Employee Recruitment
Startup Capital
Employee Mentoring
Servant Leadership
Human Resources
Team Building
Funnel Building

About the Publisher

Accepting manuscripts in the most categories. We love to help people get their words available to the world.

Revival Waves of Glory focus is to provide more options to be published. We do traditional paperbacks, hardcovers, audio books and ebooks all over the world. A traditional royalty-based publisher that offers self-publishing options, Revival Waves provides a very author friendly and transparent publishing process, with President Bill Vincent involved in the full process of your book. Send us your manuscript and we will contact you as soon as possible.

Contact: Bill Vincent at rwgpublishing@yahoo.com www.rwgpublishing.com

www.ingramcontent.com/pod-product-compliance
Lightning Source LLC
Chambersburg PA
CBHW030537210326
41597CB00014B/1180